Energy

ENERGY

Simple Experiments for Young Scientists

Larry White

illustrated by Laurie Hamilton

The Millbrook Press
Brookfield, Connecticut

This book is dedicated to our first
granddaughter, Jeanette Marie White.
She has enough energy to keep the entire
White clan hopping! Thanks for being, Jeanette.

Published by The Millbrook Press
2 Old New Milford Road, Brookfield, Connecticut 06804

Library of Congress Cataloging-in-Publication Data
White, Laurence B.
Energy : simple experiments for young scientists / by Larry White.
p.   cm.
Includes bibliographical references and index.
Summary: Through simple experiments, readers learn about
the properties of energy.
ISBN 1-56294-473-8
1. Force and energy—Experiments—Juvenile literature.   2. Power
(Mechanics)—Experiments—Juvenile literature.   3. Power resources
—Experiments—Juvenile literature.   [1. Force and energy—
Experiments.   2. Power (Mechanics)—Experiments.   3. Power
resources—Experiments.   4. Experiments.]   I. Title.   II. Series.
QC73.4.W473   1995   531.6'078—dc20   94-9836   CIP   AC

Here's a challenge: Take some energy, put it in an envelope and mail it to a friend. When your friend opens the envelope, the energy should come whirling out.

Can you do this?

If you can't imagine how this is possible, read on. You will learn how to do this later in this book. But first, exactly what is **energy?**

Energy and Work

If you ask a scientist what energy is you will be told: Energy is the ability to do **work.** Work is moving something from one place to another.

To move anything—that is, to do work—requires energy. So, energy and work go together.

Here's an experiment to illustrate how energy and work are related.

How to Do Your Homework Without Opening a Book!

Needed:

your homework notebook

Homework is work that you do at home. To do your home *work*, simply lift up your book and move it someplace else! Sure this is a silly "experiment," but it illustrates what work is: Moving the book *was* doing work, and to do this work you had to use a little of your energy. Where did you get that energy? From the food you ate. But where did the food get its energy? From the sun!

Energy Comes From the Sun

As you will learn from reading this book, there are many forms of energy. The amazing thing is that all forms of energy, except for atomic, can be traced back to the sun. To show how this happens, let's trace the energy that you used to move your homework book in the experiment you just did.

Let's say that for breakfast you had some cereal with milk and sugar and a glass of orange juice. Cereal, sugar, and orange juice all come from plants. Plants need four things to grow: warmth, water, air, and sunlight. (Most plants also need soil. Some, however, can grow without soil. Growing plants without soil is known as **hydroponics.**) The sunlight, in fact, gives them both light and warmth. With all of these a plant will grow and produce food. The sun's energy changes into chemicals inside the plants in a process known as **photosynthesis.** Photosynthesis enables plants to produce food. When you ate the products of these plants, their stored chemical energy passed on to you.

What about the milk on your cereal? Milk is not a plant. Milk comes from cows. Cows have to eat grass to stay alive. Some of the grass a cow eats also is used to produce its milk. Grass is a plant and therefore grows because the sun gives it energy. So even the energy in the milk came from the sun. That's how you can trace energy back to the sun. When you read about other forms of energy later in this book, try to trace them back to the sun, too.

Finally, of course, you passed a little of that "sun energy" to your homework book when you moved it. It all sounds quite complicated, but you have just learned a basic fact about energy: *Energy is easy to pass along from one thing to another.*

Let's explore how the sun helps plants make food with an experiment.

Plants Need the Sun's Energy to Make Food

Most plants are green because they contain **chlorophyll.** Chlorophyll is a green substance that a plant produces when it receives sunlight. Chlorophyll absorbs sunlight and helps the plant make food. (Once the plant makes food, we can then use the plant itself for food.) To make food, chlorophyll needs not only sunshine but also water and carbon dioxide from the air. What happens when you take one of these three things away?

Needed:

a green plant

aluminum foil

patience

1. Tear off a few small sheets of aluminum foil and wrap them around a few leaves of your green plant. Fold the sheets so they completely cover the leaves. No sunlight should reach the covered leaves. (See Figure 1.)

2. Wait five days and uncover the leaves.

Figure 1

What happened? Unlike the leaves around them, the leaves that were covered are no longer green. They are yellow. Without sunlight, the plant was unable to produce chlorophyll in these leaves. Without chlorophyll, the leaves could not make food. We, in turn, would not be able to use these leaves for food.

Fossil Fuels

Fossil fuels are an important source of energy that can be traced back to the sun. Fossil fuels are coal, natural gas, and oil, which is used to make gasoline.

These fuels can be traced back to the sun because they come from trees and plants that used sunlight when they lived long ago in prehistoric times. As these trees and plants died, they fell to the ground, where their remains piled up over many thousands of years. As this pile grew larger, the remains at the very bottom became pressed together. This changed the remains. Some became a gas—natural gas. Some became a liquid—oil (which is also called petroleum). And some became a rock—coal.

We use gas, oil, and coal to power our cars, heat our homes, and run our industries. When we do, we are using the stored energy of plants that are thousands and thousands of years old. Fossil fuels are our major source of energy. Because they took so long to form, however, fossil fuels cannot be replaced once they are used up. Many scientists think that we are running out of fossil fuels. They say we have to find other sources of energy to run our world. (We'll explore some of these other sources later in this book.)

Resting and Working Energy

No matter where it comes from, we depend on energy to make things move. When energy makes things move it is called **kinetic energy.**

Energy doesn't always have to make things move, however. It can simply have the ability to move things. When energy *can* move things, but doesn't, it is called **potential energy.** One way to think of kinetic energy is as energy at work. One way to think of potential energy is as energy at rest.

Energy changes all the time from potential, or resting, energy to kinetic, or working, energy. Remember the challenge at the beginning of this book: Send some energy to a friend in a letter? Solving this challenge involves changing energy from potential to kinetic.

Let's explore how.

Send a Friend a Little Energy

Needed:

a piece of cardboard 6 by 4 inches
(15 by 10 centimeters) and no thicker
than ⅛ inch (3 millimeters)

a piece of paper 4½ inches
(11 centimeters) square

a paper clip

two rubber bands of equal size

tape

scissors

envelope and stamp (optional)

a pencil

1. Fold the cardboard in half the long way. Open it with the fold facing up and one long side facing you. Cut the front side into three equal sections of 2 inches (5 centimeters) each, creating flaps. Cut two small slits, about ½ inch (13 millimeters) each in the middle of the sections at both ends. (See Figure 2.)

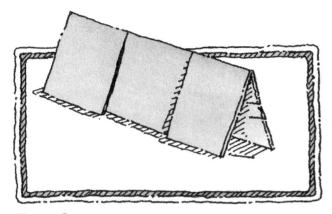

Figure 2

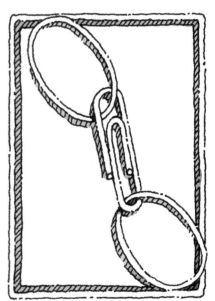

Figure 3

2. Loop the two rubber bands onto the paper clip so one is at each end. (See Figure 3.)

Figure 4

3. With your thumb, push the slits that you cut in the cardboard away from the cut edge. They should form an opening. (See Figure 4.)

4. Turn the cardboard over. Feed the rubber bands through the openings. The paper clip should be in the middle of the cardboard. (See Figure 5.)

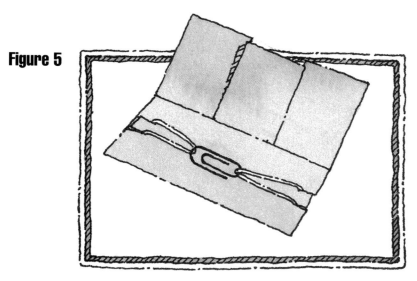

Figure 5

Figure 6

5. Fold the paper in half. Tape the bottom edges together to make a tube. On this paper print "MY ENERGY MACHINE. TAKE IT OUT TO MAKE IT WORK." (See Figure 6.)

6. Now, twist the paper clip around and around to wind up the rubber bands. Continue twisting until they are tightly wound. Before releasing the paper clip, fold the three flaps down. Hold the flaps closed so the clip can't untwist. Slip this into the paper tube, as was shown in Figure 6.

This is how you send it to your friend. When your friend pulls the cardboard out of the tube, the center flap will spring open and the bands will untwist causing the paper clip to *whirl*.

Twisting the paper clip put energy into the rubber bands. As long as the rubber bands stayed wound, that energy was unused. It was potential energy. When your friend slipped the cardboard from the tube, the rubber bands unwound and their energy was used. It changed to kinetic energy. One rule governing energy says: *Potential energy becomes kinetic energy when it is used.*

What Are Other Rules Energy Follows?

Another science rule says: *Energy can be passed from one object to another.* You saw this rule at work when you moved the book. The energy you used was transferred to you from the plant and animal food you ate. Energy was transferred to the plants (directly) and to the animals (indirectly) from the sun. Here's another activity exploring energy transference.

Pass Your Energy Along

Needed:

five nickels

a smooth table

Set four of the coins in a row on the table so they are touching one another. Lay the fifth coin 2 inches (5 centimeters) away from one end of the row. Flick this coin sharply with your finger so it slides across the tabletop and hits the fourth coin in the row. (See Figure 7.) Can you explain what happens?

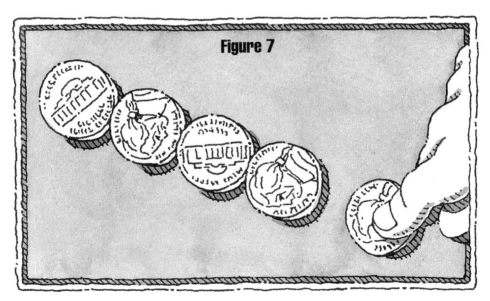

Figure 7

When you flick your finger you pass some of your energy to the fifth coin. Your energy makes it move and hit the row. When it hits, it passes the energy to the fourth coin in the row and stops. The fourth coin moves just a bit, and passes the energy to the third coin, which passes the energy to the second coin, which passes the energy to the first coin. The first coin uses the energy to move and slides across the table. (See Figure 8 on the facing page.) Your energy passes through every single coin.

Now try the experiment again, but this time flick two coins against a row of three coins. Can you explain what happens?

A bit later in this book you will be investigating the different forms energy can take. You will read how one form can change into another form. This is because of another energy rule: Energy can change from one kind to another.

Here is a simple example. Two kinds of energy are chemical and mechanical. You change chemical into mechanical energy all the time. Your food contains chemical energy, which you store in your body. If you go outside and ride a bicycle, you are making mechanical energy. After a long ride you may be hungry because your muscles have used your food (chemical) energy to make the bicycle move (mechanical energy). Your muscles simply changed one form of energy into another.

Figure 8

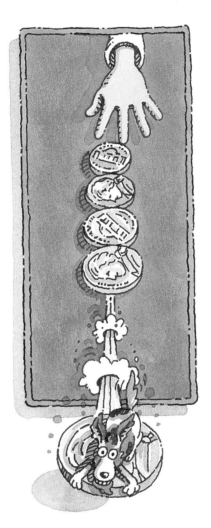

Even when you stretch a rubber band your body changes some of its chemical energy into mechanical energy. But here is a surprise. It also changes some of your energy into heat! Here's how:

Change Chemical Energy
. . . Into Mechanical Energy . . .
Into Heat Energy

Needed:

a rubber band

1. Touch the rubber band to your lips. Note its temperature (warm, cool, etc.).

2. Stretch the rubber band while still holding it to your lips. What happens? The band feels cool before it stretches, and warm while being stretched!

3. Try stretching the band quickly several times while it touches your lips. You will feel it go from cool to warm to cool to warm over and over.

Each time you stretch the band you change a tiny bit of your body's chemical energy into heat. The rubber band's temperature change is, however, very slight. Your lips are very sensitive and can detect this change. But if you stretched the rubber band without keeping it in contact with your lips, you would notice no temperature change.

What Are Some Common Forms of Energy?

As we've said, energy can take many forms. Let's meet six of the most important forms of energy. There is an easy way to remember what they are. Just remember the word *scream*. Each of the letters in *scream* is the first letter of one of the forms of energy:

$$s = sound$$
$$c = chemical$$
$$r = radiant$$
$$e = electrical$$
$$a = atomic$$
$$m = mechanical$$

Let's examine each of these forms of energy and do an experiment with each, except for atomic. Sometimes you will have to change other forms of energy into the form you wish to use in your experiment, but it is easy to do. And remember, because energy is being able to do work (move things), each of these forms of energy must be able to make something move.

Sound Energy

Sound energy makes eardrums move. Sound is made from mechanical energy. An object moves back and forth quickly and causes the air to vibrate. The vibrations travel to your ear and cause your eardrum to vibrate. Tiny nerves in your ear then send messages to your brain, and you hear the sound.

Here is an experiment that is fun and it has lots of energy changes in it. You must use your body's chemical energy to make mechanical energy to make a very funny sound.

Chicken in a Cup

Needed:

a paper or Styrofoam cup

a piece of string about 15 inches
(38 centimeters) long

a paper clip

a sharp pencil

a small piece of paper towel

water

1. Turn the cup upside down. Use the pencil to poke a small hole in the center of the bottom of the cup. Tie the paper clip on one end of the string and thread the other end of the string through the hole in the bottom of the cup. Pull it completely through until the paper clip hits the outside of the bottom of the cup. (See Figure 9.)

2. Wet the paper towel with water and wring it out so it is damp.

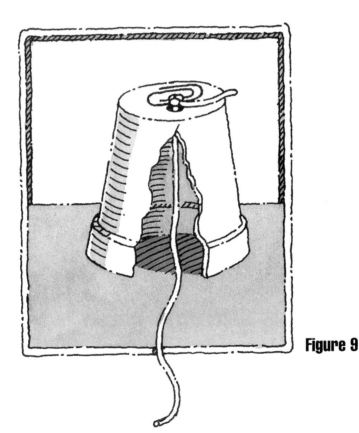

Figure 9

Figure 10

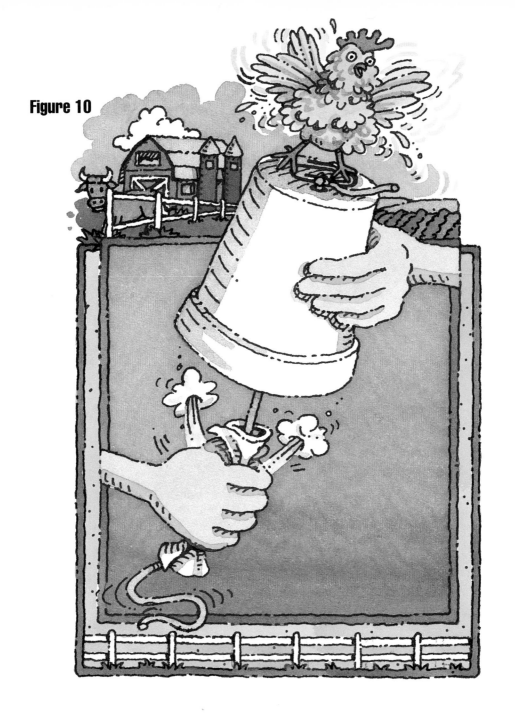

3. Hold the cup in one hand. With the other, wrap the damp towel around the string near the cup. Now, while squeezing the towel against the string, pull it downward. You will hear a loud *cluck* come from the cup. Continue pulling downward, giving short, quick yanks on the string. With a little practice you will be able to make it sound exactly like a chicken! (See Figure 10.)

People will laugh when they hear your Chicken in a Cup. But remember, all they are laughing at is the sound energy making their eardrums vibrate.

If you use the word *scream* to remember the different energy forms, it will also help you to remember that a scream is an example of sound!

Chemical Energy

Chemicals certainly can make things move. If you put a stick of dynamite, which contains the chemical compound nitroglycerin, under a big rock, the big rock will move!

Most of the energy people are concerned with is chemical energy. Coal, oil, natural gas, and gasoline are all chemicals. Food is made of chemicals. You are made of chemicals. It is simple to turn chemical energy into moving energy: You are doing it while reading this book right now by moving your eyes and turning pages.

For fun, here's how to use some common chemicals in your kitchen to make a model of one of nature's most powerful energy shows—a volcano.

Make a Kitchen "Volcano"

Needed:

a tablespoon

a coffee cup

water

baking soda

dishwashing liquid

vinegar

1. Fill the cup half full of water and set it in the sink (because this will be a bit messy), or in a large bowl. Stir in 4 tablespoons of baking soda. Add the dishwashing liquid until the cup is three quarters full.

2. To cause an "eruption," pour in vinegar until the cup is nearly full. (See Figure 11.)

Figure 11

What happened? The chemical energy was stored in the baking soda and vinegar. When these two chemicals combined they produced bubbles of carbon dioxide gas, which normally are released quickly into the air. The dishwashing liquid helped trap the bubbles and slowed their release. This created the gushing effect that resembled lava in a real volcano. (See Figure 12, page 28.)

Figure 12

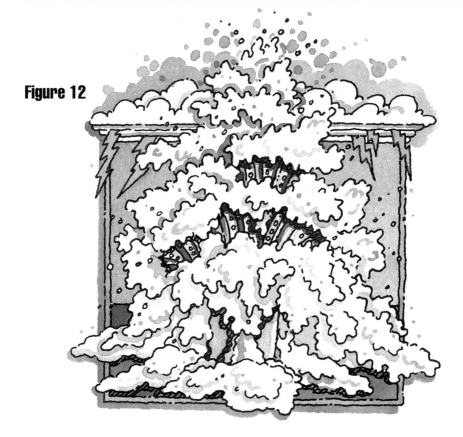

Radiant Energy

Radiant energy is actually made up of two forms of energy: heat and light. Since these forms always go together it's convenient to combine them under the single name *radiant energy.*

Fires, light bulbs, burning gas, fireflies, sparks, and even fireworks give off radiant energy. Radiant energy is also the sun's form of energy. Sunlight is by far Earth's largest source of radiant energy. When radiant energy comes from the sun it is called **solar energy.** Without solar energy everything on Earth would be frozen solid and there would be no life.

Solar energy may become even more important in our future as our fossil fuels become used up. Even today some people are using the sun's energy to heat water and warm their houses.

You probably have seen houses, or pictures of houses, with **solar collectors** on their roofs. Solar collectors are devices designed to trap the sun's radiant energy for use. Have you ever wondered how a solar collector works?

Solar collectors catch radiant energy through two means. One is by being colored black inside. Let's explore why.

Make a Hot or Cold Mitt

Needed:

aluminum foil, 5 by 12 inches
(13 by 30 centimeters)

black poster paint and a paintbrush

a sunny day (even in winter!)

1. Fold the aluminum foil in half down the middle making two 5-by-6-inch (13-by-15-centimeter) halves. Turn it so the fold is away from you. Fold over the edges of the right and left sides to make a flat bag with the bottom open. Paint the side

Figure 13

that's up black, and leave the other side silvery. You should be able to slip your hand inside, as with a mitten. (See Figure 13.)

2. Take your "solar mitt" outdoors and put it over your hand. Face the silvery side toward the sun. Your hand will feel cool inside. Next, turn your hand over so the black side faces the sun. Your hand will get hot very quickly. (See Figure 14.)

Did turning the mitt from one side to the other help you to understand this solar energy rule? *Dark-colored things absorb (take in) solar energy, and light-colored things reflect (bounce away) solar energy.* That was why your hand felt

Figure 14

warmer when the black side faced the sun. You will use this fact about radiant energy to make the solar collector in the next project.

You would find the second means of catching solar energy in a greenhouse. A greenhouse is made of transparent glass, which solar energy can pass through to reach the plants inside. As light passes through glass, it loses energy. The weaker light energy becomes, the more it is converted into heat energy. The glass panes of a greenhouse trap this heat energy, which is why a greenhouse always feels warm.

Catch Some Rays in a Solar Collector

Needed:

a cardboard box (shoe box size or larger)

scissors

clear plastic wrap

aluminum foil

tape

black poster paint and a paintbrush

a pencil

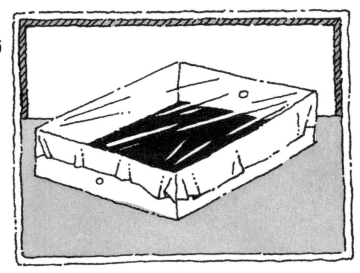

Figure 15

1. No matter what size or shape your cardboard box is, cut the top off and cut the sides so they are about 3 or 4 inches (8 or 10 centimeters) wide. (See Figure 15.)

2. With a pencil, punch a hole in the center of one of the sides and another hole in the center of the opposite side.

3. Cut a piece of aluminum foil the same size as the inside bottom of the box. Tape it to the bottom of the box (use several smaller pieces if your box is big). Paint the foil black so it will absorb radiant energy. This is called a collector plate. Its purpose is to hold the heat you catch.

4. Finally, turn your box into a "greenhouse" by covering the top with clear plastic wrap (do not cover the holes you made in the sides). Tape the wrap to the box. Your model solar collector is finished and ready for a tryout.

5. Your collector will work on any day that is sunny. Hold the collector so that one hole is up and the other down. Point the front directly into the sun. What happens?

The sunlight's radiant energy will pass through the plastic and be absorbed by the black collector plate, which will become very warm. The heat that is trapped inside cannot pass back out through the plastic, so the air inside your collector will become hot. Hot air rises. The air inside will rise to the top of the collector, and some of this hot air will come out through the upper hole. Hold your hand close to the hole, and you will be amazed to feel how hot that air is! (See Figure 16, page 35.)

If you want to try other experiments with your solar collector here are a few suggestions:

1. Use a thermometer to measure the outside temperature, then put the thermometer inside the collector to see how much hotter the solar-heated air is.

2. Lay an unpainted sheet of aluminum foil on top of your collector plate and repeat the experiment to see just how important the black color is.

3. Show how a solar collector can be used as a water heater. Put a little *cold* water in a clear plastic sandwich bag, seal the bag with a rubber band, and tape the bag against the collector plate. Replace the plastic wrap and leave your collector in the sunlight for an hour. Feel the temperature of the water.

Figure 16

4. Show how a solar collector can cook food. Paint a small square of aluminum foil black on one side and wrap it (silver side in) around a small piece of raw hot dog. Tape this against the collector plate, replace the plastic wrap, and leave your solar collector in the sunlight for an hour. Then open the foil package. (Watch out! It will be hot.) Check to see if the hot dog is cooked by noting if the skin is broken and bubbly. Enjoy eating your first "solar-cooked hot dog".

Other suggestions:

5. Try making a larger solar collector.
6. Try boxes of different shapes.
7. Add more layers of aluminum foil to hold more heat.
8. Color the collector plate different colors.

Electric Energy

Electricity is a very powerful and important form of energy. Think of all the jobs it can do for us: make heat, make cold, make sounds, make motors turn, make light, run televisions, and so many more. Even our nerves and our brains work on electricity.

Let's do a simple experiment showing how electric energy can make something move. We will use static electricity, which we can make ourselves.

Make a Puffed-Rice "Scooter"

Needed:

A piece of stiff clear plastic, about 4 by 4 inches
(10 by 10 centimeters) or larger (for example,
the lid of a margarine or cottage cheese
container or any similar packaging)

a piece of puffed-rice breakfast cereal

a tissue

1. Lay the plastic flat on the table. Rub it hard all over with the tissue. (See Figure 17.) Static electricity is produced when you rub the tissue against the plastic. You are changing mechanical energy into electric energy. You won't be able to

Figure 17

see the static electricity on the plastic, but the piece of puffed rice will show you where it is.

2. Lift the plastic sheet off the table, holding it by a corner. Drop the piece of puffed rice on the plastic. (See Figure 18.) If there is a lot of electricity, the puffed rice will jump right off the plastic as though it were a grasshopper. If there is less electricity, it will cling to the plastic. Either way, static electricity is what makes the puffed rice move. If nothing at all happens, go back to step 1 and rub a little harder and longer.

3. If the puffed rice clings, push it around the surface with your fingertip (See Figure 19.) Each time it comes near a "charge" of static electricity, it scoots over and clings to it.

Figure 18

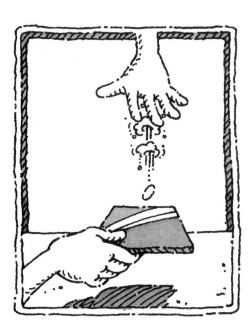

Figure 19

Atomic Energy

The entire world, and everything in it, is made of **atoms.**
Atoms are the smallest units of matter. Atoms are held together by a very powerful type of energy called atomic energy. Scientists have learned how to split atoms and release
some of this energy. Engineers are able to use the energy from
atoms to make electricity at atomic power plants.

But atomic power can also be very dangerous. In war
atomic bombs can destroy entire cities. Some people worry
about an accident happening at an atomic power plant that
might release enough energy to destroy everything around it.
And such accidents have happened. Atomic energy is the
most powerful form of energy that people have learned to
use. It is also the most dangerous. We certainly will not be
doing any experiments with atomic energy in this book.

Mechanical Energy

The last letter in *scream* represents the most familiar kind of energy: mechanical, or moving, energy. This is energy "showing itself off," and it is the one form of energy you can always identify. Whenever you see something move it has mechanical energy. A good mind exercise is this: Find something moving, then try to figure out what other form of energy besides mechanical made it move. There is always an answer.

Let's finish our study of energy with a bang. Let's use the last letter in *scream* to make the first letter. In other words, let's change mechanical energy into sound energy.

How to Make a Soda-Pop Cannon

Needed:

an empty *plastic* soda bottle, any size,
with no cap (**Warning:** Be sure to use
only a plastic bottle, never glass!)

a paper towel

1. Roll the paper towel into a tight ball, and try to fit the ball into the mouth of the soda bottle. If it is too big, unroll it and use less paper. If it is too small, roll more paper around it. You want a paper ball that fits tightly in the neck of the bottle. It is the right size when you have to force it in. (See Figure 20.)

2. With the paper ball in place, set the bottle down on its side on a table. Turn the bottle so that the neck is facing away from you.

3. Hold the wide end of the bottle with one hand. Make a fist with your other hand and slam down hard on the uppermost side of the bottle. (See Figure 21.) The "empty" bottle is

Figure 20

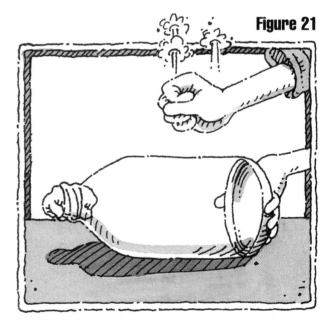

Figure 21

Figure 22

actually filled with air. When the bottle flattens, the air is forced out. It pushes the ball with it. (See Figure 22, page 42.) The ball will shoot across the room and you will hear a loud *pop*.

The slam of your fist is a perfect example of how the chemical energy you get from food changes to mechanical energy. And the *pop* you hear demonstrates how mechanical energy changes to sound energy. If anyone asks you what you are doing, don't tell them you are shooting an air gun. Tell them you are a young scientist experimenting with energy.

Glossary

atoms   the smallest units of matter

chlorophyll   a green substance that absorbs sunlight and allows plants to make food

energy   the ability to do work

fossil fuels   oil, coal, and natural gas; formed from plant and tree remains

hydroponics   the science of growing plants without soil

kinetic energy   energy that makes things move; working energy

photosynthesis   the process in which sunlight is changed to chemicals in plants, enabling them to produce food

potential energy   energy with the ability to make things move; also called resting energy

solar collectors   devices designed to trap the sun's radiant energy for use

solar energy   radiant energy that comes from the sun

work   the transference of energy when a force produces a movement in a body; moving something from one place to another

Further Reading

Adler, David. *Wonders of Energy.* Mahwah, New Jersey: Troll Associates, 1983.

Breitter, Herta S. *Fuel and Energy.* Milwaukee: Raintree-Steck-Vaughn, 1987.

Langley, Andrew. *Energy.* New York: Franklin Watts, 1986.

Murphy, Bryan. *Experiment with Movement.* Minneapolis: Lerner, 1991.

Ward, Alan. *Experimenting with Energy.* New York: Chelsea House, 1991.

Index

About the Author

In the first grade Larry White became fascinated with magic, and in high school he became fascinated with science.

Today, Larry is director of the Needham Elementary Science Center in Massachusetts, where he has taught young children for the last twenty-nine years. Before that, he was employed by the Education Department of Boston's Museum of Science. Larry has written a dozen books for curious young scientists.

Larry is also the magic editor of the magazine of the Society of American Magicians. He creates and describes magic tricks for professional magicians. He has also written over a dozen books for curious young magicians.

Larry believes that his interests in magic and science go together because things that appear magical can often be explained scientifically—if people are curious and willing to experiment and investigate.